DOLLHOUSE
DECORATING

DOLLHOUSE DECORATING

A Guide to Interior Design in Miniature,
in Twelve Distinctive Styles

NICK FORDER

COURAGE
BOOKS

With special thanks to
Charlotte Hunt, Sarah Salisbury, Muriel Hopwood, Blackwells of Hawkwell,
the staff and team of *International Dolls' House News*
and especially to Esther, my wife.

Library of Congress
Cataloging-in-Publication Number
93-74692

ISBN 1–56138–439–9

This book was designed and produced by
Quintet Publishing Limited
6 Blundell Street
London N7 9BH

Creative Director: Richard Dewing
Designer: Isobel Gillan
Project Editor: Helen Denholm
Photographer: Jeremy Thomas

Additional photographs supplied by:
Richard Bryant/Arcaid: p.37 (top); p.39 (bottom)
Ken Kirkwood/Arcaid: p.45 (bottom middle); p.49 (bottom right);
p.66 (bottom)
Rupert Cavendish Antiques: p.76 (bottom left); p.78 (top right)
Christie's Images: p.43 (bottom); p.55 (top); p.60 (middle left)
Colonial Williamsburg Foundation: p.13 (top)
J. Guillot/Edimedia: p.60 (bottom left)
E.T. Archive: p.19 (top right); p.25 (bottom)
National Trust Photographic Library: p.32 (bottom)
Donald Cooper/Photostage: p.19 (bottom right)

Typeset in Great Britain by
Central Southern Typesetters, Eastbourne
Manufactured in Singapore by Bright Arts (Singapore) Pte Ltd
Printed in China by Leefung-Asco Printers Limited

Published by Courage Books
an imprint of Running Press Book Publishers
125 South Twenty-second Street
Philadelphia, Pennsylvania 19103–4399

Contents

Introduction

THE FASCINATING HOBBY of recreating houses and their contents in detailed miniature is by no means a recent one. It has been in existence for centuries in one form or another. The earliest recorded replica of a fully furnished house was owned by Albert V, Duke of Bavaria, in the mid-sixteenth century. Following his example, many other wealthy people began to commission fine miniature pieces – both houses and their contents – to be made by expert craftsmen using all manner of different materials. These were not made for use as childish playthings, but were solely a display of taste, wealth, and social standing.

This fashion continued throughout the seventeenth and eighteenth centuries, and gradually the joy of miniatures began to be shared by the children of these wealthy households. Initially they were not so much toys as aids to education in life and household management. Nevertheless, by the mid-nineteenth century, the dollhouse was at last a plaything, though only for the children of the wealthy, and no well-equipped nursery was complete without one.

The arrival of the Victorian age saw the beginning of mass production. From then on, the dollhouse was truly a toy, and it was for this market that miniature pieces were produced in quantity. A major center of manufacture was Germany, from where dollhouse items were exported all over the world.

However, there were two notable adult exceptions to this new trend. The first was Queen Mary, the wife of King George V of England, who had a strong interest in dollhouses. In the early 1920s, one of the foremost architects of the day, Sir Edwin Lutyens, was commissioned to build a superb dollhouse for the Queen's personal pleasure. A model house was designed in the precise scale of one inch to the foot and again, as in the preceding centuries, fine craftsmen of the day were involved in the production of all manner of miniature items.

At about the same time in the United States, Mrs. James W. Thorne, a socialite from Chicago, was collecting miniatures from all over the world. She developed the idea of displaying these treasures in sets of boxes which were furnished in a variety of different styles and periods. By 1940 Mrs. Thorne had put together over forty individual room settings showing both European and American interior designs and decoration. All of these rooms were completed in exact one inch to the foot scale.

Since then, the manufacture of toy miniatures for children's dollhouses has continued and, although antique dollhouse pieces have long been collected by enthusiasts, it was not until the 1970s that adults again started to collect contemporary pieces and display them in houses or room boxes of their choosing.

Today the hobby of miniatures and miniature collecting is enjoying huge popularity, and there are a growing number of specialist shops, miniatures fairs, and dollhouse publications to cater for this interest. Miniature enthusiasts like to recreate past eras or present events in either whole houses or specific scenes. Some enjoy making the models themselves, while others collect craftsman-made pieces or commission them to be made to their particular requirements. The aim in all this is to achieve accurate detail to capture the right mood, character, and style and to add personal touches to the work, raising the hobby to an art form of creative expression.

THE INSPIRATION

The idea for a miniature creation can be taken from all manner of sources. An historic building, a family event, a fond memory, or a wild flight of imagination – all can be achieved in miniature. Within the confines of a scaled-down interior, it is possible to control all aspects of decoration, furnishing, and style, providing an environment that is an ideal world for the creator. The creation of such worlds can be true escapism, and for many miniaturists it is exactly that.

In this book we concentrate on a number of varied interiors inspired by both real life and imagination and, with simple analysis, show how the essence of each one is interpreted and recreated in miniature. There are plenty of ideas on decorating rooms and settings in a small scale. The finished miniature rooms are shown in great detail, and the approach demonstrating how each one was achieved is explained. With their diverse mix of techniques and styles, they offer a host of ideas and a source of reference and inspiration.

SIZE AND SCALE

When setting a miniature scene, a variety of aspects must be considered. Take for example the question of size. A whole street scene, a cathedral or a model of the White House is obviously going to take up considerable space. A 1:12 scale miniature can be set in a small dollhouse, a single-story shop, a room box, an open scene set under a glass dome, or even a shallow vignette behind a picture frame that can be hung on a wall. Remember that even if the scene you want to portray is large, for example a church wedding or a busy market, it is always possible to capture its flavor by focusing on an intimate detail, like the bride and groom at the altar steps or a customer at a farmer's market.

The main scale currently used is that of one inch to the foot (1:12 scale), but working smaller can solve problems of space. It is also important to consider your budget. Is a collection of the finest miniatures from top craftsmen required, or can a more accurate atmosphere be achieved by making everything yourself? Today there is a wide range of 1:12 scale miniatures available. A great number of these are quite inexpensive, but are nevertheless well detailed. With a little imagination, time, and care, these can be refashioned, repainted, and reupholstered into truly individual pieces.

THE PLANNING STAGE

An important aspect to consider is the amount of making, decorating, and assembling you can do yourself. Endless materials are available from retail specialists: scale wood moldings, roofing and floor finishes, wallpapers, door handles, light fixtures, and much more. Every conceivable requirement can be found.

For a truly successful scene, the approach should be consistent. A fine craftsman-made piece of silver very rarely looks good displayed on a basic piece of mass-produced furniture. Similarly, a room that has been carefully put together looks odd with an out-of-scale china doll standing stiffly or trying to sit within it.

It is always best to think of every detail in advance and consider each room as a whole. For example, before the Santa Fe-style furniture and accessory store (page 68) was built, a collection of miniature Southwestern items had already been started. The handpainted work of the American artists who made them, trading under the names Little White Dove and Mini Moons Ago, is very fine and specific study, and a certain talent would have been needed to create items that could blend with them. So further pieces were bought or commissioned until enough were gathered together to create the whole room. The interior was then formed simply as a backdrop to the furniture, utilizing plain terracotta tiles and wooden boards for the floor and basic colors taken from the pieces themselves for the walls. In this case, the pieces of furniture dictated the route to the finished setting.

If, on the other hand, you wish to use only pieces you have made yourself, the detail and finish of the room will be determined by the skill of the creator!

Finally, the real key to a successful miniature is good research and reference and a clear understanding of the original inspiration. It is always advisable to gather up photographs or pictures and to draw out ideas before starting. Always measure things out carefully and double-check all dimensions. Good pictures to work from and clear plans formulated at the outset are the solid foundations of a successful and rewarding result.

SELECTING A STYLE

Selecting a style in which to work might not always be easy. However, recreating an aspect of your own life has advantages in that the time and setting of that theme will have already been set. This may be the place to start!

When commissioning a miniature reproduction of her husband's first restaurant, the wife of a successful restaurateur had no problem in deciding questions of style. Built in the hillside south of Los Angeles, this early fast food place had all the modernity of the early 1940s. Copied from early photographs and relying on keen memories, the miniature model revived it all. From the bar with stools to the separated booths and all the latest equipment behind the counter, every aspect was recreated. The whole model was designed and built by expert miniaturists Pat and Noel

7

Thomas. Since they made everything, from the shelves on the walls to the shingles on the roof, total unity was guaranteed. Being built in the scale of one inch to the foot (1:12), it was then possible to purchase well-chosen foods, drinks, and accessories to complete the project.

The building of this restaurant was an involved job. It entailed recreating both an interior and an exterior as an exact replica which is obviously a time-consuming task. For a first project it may be advisable to start with a ready-made box or room and concentrate solely on one or two interiors. For the projects in this book, we have done just that and in the main have used boxes with floor measurements of about 12 × 20 inches (30 × 50cm).

Smaller boxes could clearly be used, but remember that for good viewing the depth of a room should only be just over half the width. Within this space, walls can be added and floors raised to break away from the conformity of the box. Once you are at this stage, pieces of furniture can be tested in various positions, and the plan for the room layout begins to take shape.

TOOLS AND MATERIALS

When the project has been chosen, there are basic materials and tools to assemble. Photographs and drawings should already be on hand together with pencils, erasers, a ruler, steel tape measure, and scissors. A small modeler's saw and miter block are both great assets, but the real essentials are a sharp craft knife and metal cutting edge, small paint and art brushes, a drill, small screwdrivers, a jigsaw, a soldering iron, needle-nosed pliers, a tack hammer, and assorted sizes of sandpaper.

Today a wide variety of adhesives and glues are available; by and large, there is one for each specific purpose, and these do not change because the work is in miniature. You will need wallpaper paste, wood glue, fabric adhesive, instant glue, and an all-purpose glue for cardboard and other lightweight materials.

The materials required depend largely on the project. However, several separate purchasing trips will be saved if you keep in stock a small can of white vinyl silk latex

paint, fine surface crack filler, a sheet of mounting cardboard, and a sheet of ¹⁄₁₆-inch (1.5mm) basswood.

If it is your intentioin to construct a whole building or an exterior as well as an interior, clear plans will have to be drawn up, and the quantity of plywood or composite board calculated. For most miniature projects, a thickness of between ¼ and ½ inch (6–12mm) is usually suitable, and if you are working with plywood, one faced with birch is favorable because it has a finer surface.

A WORK SCHEDULE

Once you have planned the basic construction, think next about the miniatures themselves. The interior you have planned may require you to make everything yourself. Plot this carefully and work out every aspect, listing the materials that need to be found or bought. When you are at this stage of planning, a trip to a specialist miniature shop or show might be a good idea, if at all possible. Purchasing some ready-made items may save a lot of unnecessary work and indeed can form the nucleus of the scheme itself.

Finished pieces can then be placed and tested within the working space. Often larger pieces of furniture work better positioned toward the back of the room with smaller ones toward the front. When planning lighting, lamps positioned within the back half of the room will have the greatest effect.

Finally, before starting work, plan a course of action. As with building and decorating a real house, there must be an ordered sequence of activity. For all the projects in this book, a basic order of work was followed, which adheres to the sequence described below.

First, all construction work must be completed – floors, walls and ceiling put in place and doorways, arches, and windows cut. You should consider whether you want chimney breasts and false walls at this stage.

Second, plan the wiring. Pre-position the lights by holding the light fixtures in place and marking their position. Run the wire or special copper tape behind undecorated walls and ceilings or across the bare floor.

Third, start decorating. Paint the ceiling and walls and follow on with papering if required. Miniature cornices, architraves, and baseboards can be finished separately and fitted at this stage.

Fourth, connect the lighting, insert the floor, and check that all construction work is complete.

Finally, dress the window, arrange the furniture, and add accessories. These can all be adjusted until exactly the right effect is achieved.

ABOVE

A sidelong view of some of the seating and tables in an early California fast-food restaurant made by miniature specialists Pat and Noel Thomas. Standard 1:12 scale accessories were carefully chosen.

LEFT

The counter and bar stools inside the restaurant. The coffee maker and other glass items were made especially for the project.

American Colonial Living Room

T he style of this room, now more popularly known as "country," captures all the romance of the life of the early American settlers. This is an immensely popular style, and those lucky enough to own an early home often feel that accurate restoration and sympathetic furnishings are essential to maintain a true balance. This miniature probably represents a room within a newer building where furniture and objects of a bygone age have been gathered together to recreate the charming simplicity of an older home.

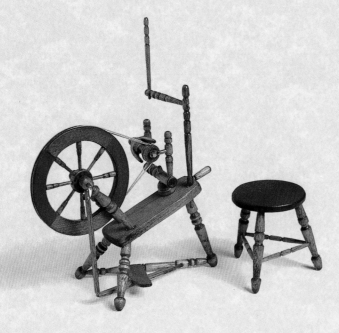

RIGHT

A miniature two-door pie safe, containing assorted handcrafted pies. It is made mainly of wood. The metal panel doors were pierced with small holes, and the rough edge faces outward, both to allow air to circulate and to deter flies and insects from flying in!

Some years after their arrival in North America, the first pilgrims progressed to building more substantial houses than their early crude shelters made of mud. By the beginning of the eighteenth century, these had been replaced by sturdier buildings.

They used whatever local materials were available and made adaptations to suit their needs, but even so their old homes in England were very much the example. In this type of combination room, which was both a kitchen and a living room like an old English parlor, the fireplace was the most important feature as it was used both for cooking and heating. As in England, ceilings were low to conserve heat, and windows were small and few. Furnishings were sparse; ladderback chairs, settles, and tilt-top tables were all common; in fact, anything that could be was copied from the memory of life back home. Today early colonial pieces are

This is a kitchen interior at Carter's Grove, run by the Colonial Williamsburg Foundation. In the center of the room is a large wooden table flanked by trestle benches with two large hutches standing against the walls. Note the spinning wheel – an essential tool – and the huge fireplace with flatirons ranged along the mantelpiece.

BELOW

The miniature living room in colonial style.

much sought after for homes that recreate the style of early American country life.

A hardwood, boarded floor with oval rag rugs, a planked and beamed low ceiling, white walls, and an open fire – these are the features that form the basis of an early Colonial room.

Walls were usually white, but other colors were also used: deep green, blue, and even rust red. These colors, too, were used for woodwork and painted furniture. Distinctive forms of furniture are the topped hutch and the pie safe with its pierced tin front to repel flies and other insects.

The fireplace, if used for cooking as well, would have had a brick insert and would be fully furnished with the relevant ironwork. Simple candle lighting and country tools and equipment are all key elements needed to set the scene. This miniature room was constructed and furnished with thoughts in mind of what furniture and implements would have been in use at that time.

The window is set back in a deep wall behind the fireplace, and the door, the baseboards, and fire surround are painted a deep thicket green. A "witch's hat" five-arm chandelier was chosen for the lighting for the room. Standing beside the brick-lined fireplace there is a spinning wheel, a washboard, and handpainted wall cupboard. In the center of the mantelpiece is a miniature piece of chalkware. Chalkware was an imitation of real porcelain pieces, bought when the original could not be afforded. There

13

To make this interior, a room box with one side completely open was chosen in which to create the scene. First of all, a substantial chimney breast was constructed and an opening for the fire was cut. This was made slightly larger than the interior of the fire surround, which had been bought ready made. In the side wall beyond the fire, another hole was cut to accommodate a window frame – a location very typical of early houses. The walls were painted white and then pre-stained, and varnished boards were attached to the ceiling and ⅜-inch (1cm) "distressed beams" were overlaid at evenly spaced intervals. These, too, were stained to match the general color.

Next, ready-made miniature floorboard sheets were trimmed and glued to the floor, and the area within the fireplace was painted a stone color to represent the fire base. Miniature bricks were built up to make the fire walls and made to look dirty with black and brown paint to represent general wear.

The purchased fireplace had come with its own hearth and back, but these were removed before it was painted a deep green. This color, in turn, was slightly rubbed off as it dried to allow the original brown color of the piece to show through. Logs on andirons, an adjustable ratchet, and a cast iron cooking vessel were added last.

Miniature baseboard was painted the same green as the fireplace and then measured and mitered at the corners until it fitted neatly around the whole room. A space was left to mount the pre-painted false door to the wall.

In the case of this room, lighting was a simple matter. A single, five-arm chandelier known as a "witch's hat" was wired from a single source through the ceiling above.

Finally, the main pieces of furniture were positioned, and the quilt rack, wall shelf, Monticello kitchen bowl, and spinning wheel were added as final touches.

RIGHT

An open-topped hutch by Sir Thomas Thumb displaying a decoy duck, a candle mold, a water flask, a painted box, pitchers, and other useful vessels.

are guns in a rack above the fire, prospector's gold in a bag, candles in a box on the wall, and a six-board chest beside the door which is hand-painted in Connecticut design. All these items are ideal for such a room.

LEFT

A handpainted six-board chest in Connecticut design produced by Oldham Studios.

OPPOSITE

The false door (right), next to which stands the six-board chest and the open-topped hutch.

Egyptian Bedroom

From time to time, designers of all kinds have borrowed themes from ancient Egypt. It is a rich source of inspiration to draw upon, whether for directors of Hollywood movies, Art Deco designers, interior stylists or architects. The Egyptian room in the Harrods store in London and the lavish Las Vegas Luxor Pyramid Hotel, built in the shape of a pyramid, are two modern and very different interpretations of the Egyptian theme. The owners of the latter claim that history is about to be rewritten as they have built a new pyramid that rises some 350 feet (106m) above the Mojave Desert floor.

ODAY NEARLY ALL the artifacts from ancient Egypt we are able to see are those that have, at some time, been uncovered from a burial tomb. The most famous discoveries have been at the tomb of King Tutankhamen, found by Howard Carter in the 1920s. Since then major exhibitions of these treasures have been mounted all across the world. By looking at these artifacts, people have been able to examine the fabulous use of precious substances – gold, alabaster, ivory, bronze, copper, lapis lazuli, ebony and other exotic woods – in amazing art forms that challenge and fire the imagination.

For the miniaturist, floors of marble, walls of desert stone, the strong shapes of pyramids and pillars are the images that transport the imagination back to this ancient time. Furniture can be decorated with gold and encrusted with stones. Spectacular hieroglyphic inscriptions can be used on walls or furniture. Ornaments of Canopic jars, small mummies, and figures of priests, priestesses and dieties are other additions to help create the right atmosphere.

This room – a flirtation with Egyptian fantasy – could be anything from a stage set or a store display to Cleopatra's boudoir itself. Although it takes ideas for colors, finishes, and use of materials from the treasures uncovered in the tombs, this 1:12 scale room probably owes more of its influence to the films of Cecil B. De Mille than to the ancient Egyptians!

This wood-constructed set measuring 20 inches (50cm) deep by 24 inches (60cm) wide and 16 inches (40cm) high has a floor of solid marble. The ceiling is rough-finish plaster the color of desert sand, and around its edge there is a wide, carved cornice gilded and painted to match the colors of semiprecious stones. Behind the long, flowing, silk drapes,

BELOW

A front-on view of the whole room, which demonstrates the dramatic symmetrical arrangement.

18

This handpainted bust of the Egyptian Queen Nefertiti, who lived in the fourteenth century B.C., is the work of craftsman Neil Carter.

OF ALL THE images associated with ancient Egypt, that of the sphinx is perhaps most universally recognized. These giant stone statues standing in the desert have made generations curious about the culture that produced them.

The Egyptian theme lends itself to dramatic interpretation on stage and screen – perhaps the sheer scale of items like the sphinxes and pyramids inspire grandiose designs. The production of *Aida*, staged by the English National Opera, shown below, uses a giant mask as a backdrop.

The miniaturist may be similarly inspired. It is worth examining stage and film sets to see how designers have incorporated elements of Egyptian style, as well as looking at original paints and artifacts.

ABOVE

Taking center stage in the room is the magnificent bed. Made of carved wood, this mass-produced piece has been gilded and painted to fit the part. Antique silk gauze cascades down from the canopy, and sitting on the top of the frame is a mask of Tutankhamen.

light shines from above, and behind the bed, stone blocks with hieroglyphic inscriptions can just be seen. Light from outside the set also freely passes through it, for there are no front or side walls, only the fine silk gauze curtains, a unique feature of this miniature.

This set has been symmetrically arranged. To the right and left, behind limpid pools of water, stand gilded wooden plinths. On top of these, in exactly the same position on opposite sides of the bed, stand the bust of Queen Nefertiti and the figure of the jackal-headed god Anubis. In front of the bed are two matching Victorian brass sphinxes and also paired are two gilded wooden stools. In the foreground, facing each other on either side of the room, stand gilded, marble-topped altar tables, each crowned with treasures. On one stands a small mummy in its

open sarcophagus beside which are two amulet cats, each made of metal and gilded. Beneath it stands a Victorian bisque jar. On the other, a pair of green marble obelisks are centered by a dish of grapes.

In the center of the room on a raised marble section stands the opulent, gilded bed. Its covers are of pure white, antique crushed silk and from its canopy fall pleats of antique gauze. Gilded steps lead up to the bed on each side.

In a room of glittering gold and soft white tones, the light plays on a miniature asp escaping from its urn; this finishing touch is a subtle reminder of the tragic fate of Cleopatra.

The construction of this project was somewhat dictated by the size of marble tiles available. Marble is not easy to cut neatly, so where a measurement is arbitrary, it seemed unnecessary to stick to a predetermined size.

Two 12 × 12-inch (30 × 30-cm) tiles, side by side, made up the width, and a third tile placed on top 6 inches (15cm) from the front determined the depth. The corner spaces left uncovered could then be made into pools of water. The ceiling height was judged so that it would be in proportion with the floor size and also so that it would be tall enough to show off the bed. The set has a solid back wall 2 inches (5cm) taller than the required ceiling height, but at the front the roof is supported by two pillars.

Having textured and decorated the exterior of the box and the interior back wall, a pre-painted ceiling piece with a decorated edge was fitted into place. This measures 1 inch (2.5cm) smaller in width and ½ inch (12mm) less in depth than the overall room size. Set onto the front pillars and attached by long pins at each back corner, this false ceiling leaves a gap of ½ inch (12mm) at the back and sides for light to filter through.

Pre-pleated glass curtain, kept in shape with hair spray, was glued around the tops of the walls just above the ½-inch (12mm) gap. A 60-watt fluorescent tube was mounted above the false ceiling onto the back wall, and an overall roof was made to enclose it.

With the marble floors in place, plastic "water" sheets were fitted into the corner spaces, and two small back ledges painted a sand color were positioned behind them.

With the structure complete, attention was given to the furniture. All the pieces chosen were inexpensive and mass-produced. The two side tables originally had back mirrors which were taken off. The inappropriate seat covers on the stools and the bed linen were also removed. Then, together with the two pedestals, all were carefully sanded and treated with a three-part gilding process. On the bed and stools, carvings were picked out with suitable paint colors, while the side tables received hieroglyphic decorations.

A new mattress and bolster were made for the bed and covered with antique crushed silk. A lucky find of old gauze was draped around the canopy and allowed to fall onto the floor.

While searching for suitable inspiration for this scene, two almost-identical inkwells were found. Their heads tilt back to reveal ink pots, and these were ideal to flank the bed. With all the furniture now complete, it remained only for the other accessories to be positioned.

ABOVE
On a gilded plinth stands another of Neil Carter's pieces. This one is of the jackal-headed god, Anubis.

LEFT
A marble-topped side table displaying a small, open sarcophagus and two cat amulets. On the bottom stands a Victorian bisque jar.

Swedish Gustavian Bedroom

Light, bright rooms decorated with molded paneling picked out in gold and polished wooden floors form the essence of a Swedish Gustavian room. Each room would have contained a huge, tiled stove in either rectangular or circular form. Although these were sometimes plain, the decoration of the tiles was often truly splendid — after all, it was an important focal point. Greek motifs of swags of leaves, figurines, and flowers abounded, and ormolu and gilt was used on fixtures and furniture alike.

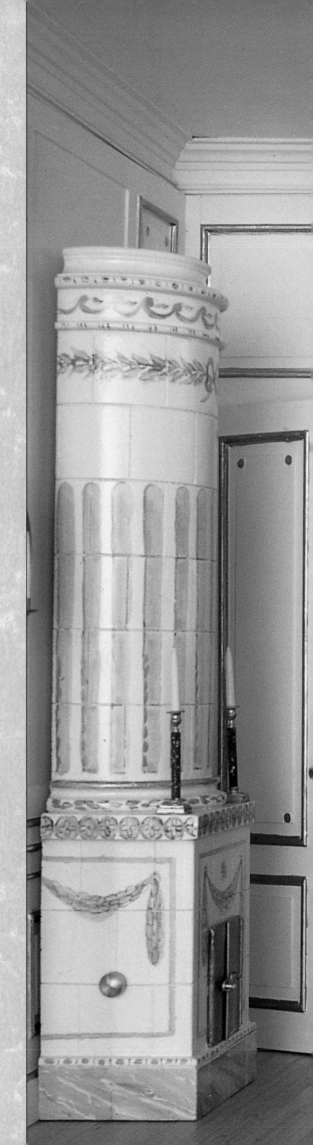

I N 1772 GUSTAV III acceded to the throne of Sweden, having just returned from a trip to France. There he had been absorbed in the art and design of the new French neoclassical style. He was determined that after many years of obscurity, Sweden should once again take its place in Europe, both politically and culturally. He believed strongly that his personal interest in the arts and the influence he could wield was all-important.

To this end, in the same year as his coronation, Gustav III commissioned Jean Eric Rehn to decorate the King's State Bedroom in the Royal Palace in Stockholm. This is thought to be the first important Gustavian room to be completed.

The link between France and Sweden continued throughout Gustav's reign. Swedish architects traveled to France, and many French craftsmen came to Sweden to teach and work. In the neoclassical style, rooms were light and fresh, and furniture was often decorated with urns, medallions, and other classical Greek motifs. French-style chairs were made with elegant oval backs. Gilding and mirrors were important features of the style, and the use of light woods and pale colors such as grays, blues, and greens made the maximum use of available light.

Based on a small bedroom designed in the early 1790s for Prince Frederick Adolf, this miniature interior is a very special room. Glancing around it, you can recognize the shapes and influences that are found in Biedermeier and Empire styles, but somehow the Gustavian style remains unique.

The design and furniture painting of this room is all the work of miniature specialist Charlotte Hunt. Of Swedish origin herself, this is a style that is near to her heart. Remaining true to the Gustavian style, the walls are all white with gilded panel moldings.

The central section behind the bed has been covered with a blue-gray silk that matches the cover of the gilded bed. The walls of the little side chambers have been covered with wallpapers, as can be seen through the open doors. The floors are of light, polished wood partly covered by a handmade rug positioned next to the bed.

One of the most distinguishing features of this type of Swedish interior is the magnificent, tall, tiled stoves. Originally they stood on wooden feet as individual pieces of furniture, but later fire laws prohibited this. The tiles of the stoves were often highly decorative, and

OPPOSITE
The huge tiled stove on one side of the bedroom. Through the partly open doors can be seen a glimpse of the room beyond.

25

AN ENTRANCE HALL from Tulgarn, Sweden. The whole atmosphere of this room, from the gold panel moldings on the walls and the large mirror, to the gilt, round-backed chairs and the tiled stove, is Swedish Gustavian. You can see how certain elements are perfectly represented in the miniature. Compare, for example, the stove, the chandelier, and the chest shown here with those in miniature.

the stove was frequently the most expensive item in the room. This one gives an almost *trompe l'oeil* effect.

Within each panel of the wall beside the stove are gilded candle holders. These have oval mirrors behind them to reflect the light back into the room.

On the right-hand wall, opposite the stove, is another huge, gilded mirror. Beneath stands a handpainted chest. Often Gustavian furniture was painted to represent special inlaid woods such as rosewoods, ebony, and others. This particular piece has also the family crest upon it, as does each item of the dressing table set laid out on the marble top.

From the ceiling hangs a glass chandelier, true to the Gustavian style. The original would have had wax candles for illumination. In front of the bed there is a small three-legged table with a silver coffee set on a tray. The painted chair alongside it has the typical oval back of the time.

Charlotte Hunt, together with her team of helpers, produced all the individual pieces in this room. Each craftsperson, through experience in a specific field, helps to produce authentic furniture of the highest quality. However, for those planning a miniature in this most elegant of Swedish styles, items can be bought or commissioned from Charlotte Hunt Miniatures, and rooms can be put together in much the same way as this charming example.

BELOW
The complete miniature interior.

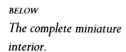

LEFT
Beyond the handpainted chest, open doors provide a view of an adjacent dressing room.

RIGHT
Handpainted "tiled" stove created by Charlotte Hunt. The chain on the right is to adjust the flue.

BELOW
Often wooden furniture was faux *painted to represent intricate inlay work. Here, in typical style, Charlotte Hunt has reproduced her own family crest on the front of the low chest.*

Georgian Kitchen

The Georgian age is associated with elegant living, at least for those who lived in the splendid wealthy homes of England. In important rooms, decorations and moldings of plaster work, curtains and large carpets, together with craftsman-made furniture all combined to give an air of calm refinement.

Not so in the kitchen. Here little had changed for two or three centuries. Set in the basement of the house, it was often cold, with little or no daylight. It was a functional place where the kitchen staff worked hard to produce cooked food for large households.

I N KITCHENS SUCH as these, the floor was of hard stones, and the solid walls would have been covered with a slim layer of plaster. Cooking methods were much the same as they had been for years. Huge open fires, sometimes with ornate iron firebacks, were used for cooking, and pots and kettles hung from cranes and hangers. The huge logs would have rested on andirons, and there would have been a roasting spit turned either by clockwork or by hand. Salted sides of bacon and other meats would be hung from the ceiling to cure, and huge hutches were used to store the dishes and utensils on open shelves, with the linen housed in the cupboards below. The plain pewter plates and china dishes would have been completely unadorned.

All baking, preserving, and food preparation was done in the kitchen, and the central wooden work table dominated the middle of the room. The general atmosphere would have been bleak. Walls were plain in color and probably grimy from the cooking. The stone floor, though scrubbed clean, offered no comfort; the emphasis was always on the work in hand. The sink would be made of stone or slate, and only cold water could be pumped through to it. All furniture would be pine, or perhaps light oak, as might be the door and window frame (if there was one). The huge fireplace would be blackened with soot, with the cooking utensils all made of cast iron or copper.

In keeping with the notion of a Georgian kitchen, this miniature model has all the ingredients to make the atmosphere just right. The floor is of irregular stones, and the walls are plastered white. A giant, open fireplace dominates the rear wall. Here, huge logs straddle the andirons, and there are more stored in a plank tub beside the fire. The smoke jack for roasting meat can be turned mechanically and also by hand. Within the brick hearth, there is an iron chimney crane with a griddle and an adjustable ratchet, hanger, hanging rails, and fireplace tools. On the front fireplace beam hangs a brass bottle jack. A pair of leather-sided bellows and a floor trivet can also be found.

In the back corner on the right is the old slate sink with one single faucet supplying cold water from outside. On the shelves above the drain board are tin-lined copper pots and a fish steamer. To the left of the fireplace are two steps up to the door that leaves the kitchen.

Against the wall to the left stands an enormous hutch. The cupboards underneath hold linens and towels, while on the shelves above, many items for cooking, eating, and storage are ready at hand. There are pewter and earthenware plates, open pie dishes, pitchers and pots, a rabbit mold, bowls, and two round cheeses.

In a kitchen of this type, most food preparation would have taken place on long central tables. On this table there are assorted vegetables, carving knives, small loaves, dishes, and a pillar of sugar. The shelf underneath was

OPPOSITE
On the floor in front of the hutch lies a broken bowl where a cook has been careless! The stone floor would have been swept with a twig broom like the one standing in the corner.

31

ABOVE
This view of the whole room shows how it is dominated by the key features – the fireplace for cooking and the table for preparing food.

LEFT
The enormous kitchen hutch displays all manner of kitchenware from earthenware pots, plates, and pitchers to pewter dishes.

provides a focal point of an English Georgian kitchen. Following directions from the modelers, Sussex Crafts, the chimneypiece was constructed from plywood, and a pre-stained beam was positioned over the opening. Brick sheets from Sussex Crafts were then used to line the internal walls.

Next the ceiling and kitchen walls were painted white and dirtied with powder paints to give the effect of age. Particular attention was paid to staining the walls around the sink, which would quickly have become splashed and grimy.

Sussex Crafts also produces sheets of miniature stones for the floor. Once these were cut and fitted, the cracks between them were grouted and stained to represent the effect of the years of collected dirt.

With the sink set into the corner, a small piece of basswood was fashioned into a drain board, and two further pieces were cut for shelves on the wall above. A light stain was then applied to them and a further wash of

ABOVE

The central kitchen table with various foodstuffs, utensils, and a pillar of sugar.

originally used for storing cooking pots.

This room is set within a plywood room box, but because of its regular shape it could just as easily have been made on the basement floor of a commercially made plywood dollhouse. Once again, internal structural work was the first job to be accomplished. As has already been established, the huge open fireplace

BELOW

On the chopping block, a duck awaits its final fate.

A NUMBER OF National Trust properties in U.K. have well-maintained Georgian kitchens of this style. This one at Saltram in

Devon has a typical fireplace with the spit above it, the hutch with rows of china, and plenty of copper pots and pans.

dirty paint rubbed over them. A ready-made false door was given the same finishing treatment, and a pair of steps lifted the door to 1½ inches (4cm) higher up on the wall.

The oversized hutch was made by adding a made-up top to a pair of plain purchased wooden bedroom cupboards, and the two tables were crudely made from basswood. Before staining and dirtying these, they were heavily sanded in order to give the effect of the age.

To complete the making stage, a short length of laurel branch was sawn off and its bark re-moved. Then bands of lead were attached around it. Because of its fine grain, it made an excellent chopping block.

The fireplace was equipped with all the nec-essary paraphernalia – all of which were pro-duced by Sussex Crafts. A dab of flat black paint on each piece dulled the shiny newness, making them look well-used.

For this miniature, quite a few accessories were bought. For the hutch, the fine ceramic ware is made by Stokesy Ware, as are the pie dish and pitcher on the main table.

The meats, pies, and cheeses are again English and made by the Lincolns. The excellent birds, whose plumage is made from real feathers, and the food on the table are the work of Sally Lambert of Busy Fingers, and the copper ware is by Jason Getzan.

ABOVE
The huge open fire, complete with smoke jack, chimney crane with griddle and adjustable ratchet hanger, hanging fireplace, and other fireplace tools. Above, the meat and a brace of birds which have been hung up to cure can be seen.

Shaker Room

S et in the style of the Shakers of 1830–50, the miniature interior of this room box depicts many of the aspects of Shaker life. For a style as specific as this, where uniformity and symmetry are the keys, it was fortunate that the furniture of just one maker – Englishman John Morgan – could be used for the whole room. To begin to understand this style, it is important to know something of the Shakers themselves and the beliefs that governed everything they did.

I T WAS IN about 1770 when Ann Lee, a working-class Englishwoman, had a vision of a simple way of religious living. She formed her United Society of Believers in the first and second appearance of Christ (named Shakers because of their dance worship), in the belief that people could live aside from human faults with Christ as a role model. Men and women would be equal, living celibate lives that were materially simple and well ordered.

Ten years later in America, amid a religious revival, Ann eventually convinced a group of Baptists to join her in her beliefs, and by 1840 there were nearly 6,000 sisters and brothers living and working in closed communities from Maine to Kentucky. Their lives were simple, but the excellence of their work was unsurpassed and the things they produced were

BELOW

This complete interior in miniature reflects the simple harmony of style achieved by the Shakers.

So the Shaker style evolved. Furniture and interiors were designed to fit this specific way of life, employing light woods and delicate unadorned shapes. This sparse, uniform furniture was made for simple, sharing, communal living.

To recreate the Shaker style, consider the following factors. Interiors should be plain, simple, and unadorned, using colors that are pure, bright, and natural. For furniture, the wood used should resemble birch, light oak or tiger maple and be fashioned into simple forms. Floors should be of bare, light wood with perhaps only an oval rag rug for comfort.

Furniture that epitomizes the Shaker style are ladderback chairs and rockers with woven seats, small three-legged work tables, narrow single beds, oval storage boxes, and a board of pegs around the walls for hanging storage.

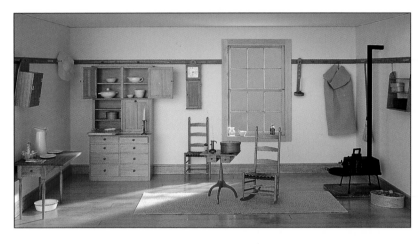

made with great thought and diligence. There was a system of education, apprenticeship, and order in everything. Uniformity and sharing were the key to the whole society, with every member receiving the same and living in the same simple way. Rooms were simply furnished and everything was kept to a minimum.

In their style of furniture, the Shakers employed the same simple rules that they applied to their lives. They used basic unadorned woods, fashioned into shapes that were pleasing to the eye. Cleanliness and tidiness were all-important, so dust-free cupboards and drawers, frequently built-in, were the order of the day.

Furniture was made for sharing, and often several pieces of the same style were produced at the same time, as this made the most practical use of time and materials.

A TRUSTEES DESK at the Hancock Shaker Village in Pittsfield, Massachusetts. At this desk, accounts would have been written up and records of outside dealings kept. The cupboards above and below were used for storing files, while pigeonholes behind the desk flaps housed letters, religious writings, and quotations. "Provide places for all your things, so that you may know where to find them at any time of day or night" is a saying attributed to Mother Ann. It epitomizes the Shaker attitude toward storage.

ABOVE

A Shaker ladderback rocking chair with a woven seat. This chair represents possibly the best-known Shaker item. It is the epitome of Shaker work; light and graceful but strong. The knobs on the back are not simply decorative but were there for the purpose of lifting it.

LEFT

This view of the room shows the miniature peg board around the wall which was used for hanging up various items. Here a small cabinet, a sun hat, and a working clock are being kept out of the way on the wall.

LEFT

A trustees desk made by John Morgan from alder wood. A desk such as this would have been shared by community leaders. The two central flaps fold down to provide the desk when needed, but at other times it can be kept closed flat to keep the insides clean and dust free.

BELOW

This bedroom or "retiring room" is again the work of John Morgan of Simply Shaker. It has a hardwood floor, hanging pegs around the wall, and a narrow, single bed with typical Shaker-style bedding.

Within this room box, the walls and ceiling are plain white, and the floor is made of cut strips of planking that have been stained and varnished. Around the walls runs the typical peg board of unevenly spaced pegs from which hang a variety of interesting items. A clock with pendulum and weights, hats, warm woolen cloaks, brushes and brooms would all be hung from these pegs. Even chairs were hung by their backs when not in use. Hanging open shelves can be used to hold the oval boxes which have now become almost an emblem of Shaker lifestyle.

These storage boxes were made in many sizes for all manner of household and workshop needs. The swallow-tailed fastening, with its small copper tacks that would not rust or discolor the wood, prohibited the wood from splitting with swelling and shrinkage.

Throughout both rooms, other pieces of furniture and accessories in keeping with the style have been included.

A three-legged sewing table containing sewing needles, pins, and threads within the small drawers stands in the main room. This would

LEFT

Standing on a slate base is a typical cast iron wood-burning stove which was much more efficient than a fireplace. Flatirons were heated on its sides, and the long stove pipe helped to distribute extra heat. An open Shaker box full of apples is beside it. The hanging candle holder can be adjusted higher or lower on the pegs to give light at just the right height.

A SHAKER STOVE from the Hancock Shaker Village in Pittsfield. Being positioned well out into the room additional heat from the stovepipe was also distributed.

have been made by a Shaker Brother for a Sister to work her craft. Against the wall there is a small drop-leaf table. On it are a pitcher, plates, and a basket for eggs, which would probably not have been made by the Shakers themselves, but traded with the outside world in return for produce of their own.

In the retiring room, a small mirror and towel rack hang from the pegs, and the washstand is completed with a pitcher and bowl. Personal cleanliness was all-important to the Shaker community.

The maker of these miniature rooms has analyzed every aspect of Shaker life and recreated many of the things that epitomized their distinctive style. The pieces have been copied extremely faithfully and, in the main, are fashioned from American cherry wood and subsequently sealed, waxed and polished. Constructed from birch plywood, the main room measures 17½ inches (44cm) wide by 10½ inches (26cm) deep and 8½ inches (20cm) high and the retiring room measures 10½ inches (26cm) square by the same height.

Victorian Gothic Bedroom

H igh in some tower or down beside a deep moat, this bedroom lies behind a thick castle wall. Is the door locked or does the occupant roam free? This room is a product of the imagination, delving deep into dark tales of haunted castles, ghostly figures, and mysterious happenings. However, from the point of view of its style, this interior is truly Victorian in its evocation of the Gothic.

F ROM 1837 TO 1901 Queen Victoria was on the British throne, giving the title "Victorian" to a time span of over sixty years. This was an era of great expansion, social change, and luxurious living. A new middle class emerged with the means to surround themselves with every finery that money could buy. The home was all-important, and its embellishment was the perfect way to show off financial achievement. In his search for every contrivance to show his opulence, the Victorian took what he considered to be the best of design and decoration from every epoch and reworked them into a powerful new style. Influenced by the strength and tradition of a bygone age, one such historical style was Gothic.

Gothic, a word meaning barbarous or crude, was the name given to medieval architecture by classicists of the eighteenth century. However, it does not really describe the magnificent engineering achievements that the Victorians admired so much in this style. In their interpretation, they incorporated everything that was medieval. Features such as high arched windows and doors and carved ornamentation, the use of basic materials of stone and dark woods, and the incorporation of rough walls and decorative ironwork have now come to be known collectively as Victorian Gothic. The furniture would typically be made in dark wood in high arched forms and with medieval decoration.

Conversely, furniture was comfortable and well upholstered, and pictures and ornaments abounded. Floors might well be stone, and the woodwork was often stained dark, but essential to the style was the ornate painted or carved decoration.

In this miniature interpretation of the style, the Victorian Gothic bedroom has dark gray walls representing large stone blocks, and the rough floor is a heavy stonework. Worn stone steps lead down from the door. At the bottom is an old suit of armor, and, as an imaginative touch, a jeweled cup of gold has been left as if knocked over.

The bedroom furniture is almost black. Note the high arched forms of the dresser and its chair and also the "cathedral window" effects in the back and foot of the bed and on the cup-

ABOVE
The dresser and chair display high arched forms that look like medieval windows. Note that there are even cathedral-like spires on top of the dresser.

OPPOSITE
This view of the room focuses on the corner staircase. The effect of rough-hewn stone steps was achieved using styrofoam blocks which were chipped, sanded, and painted.

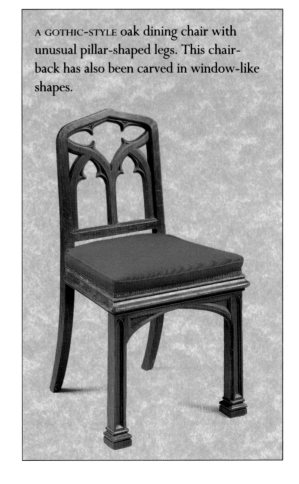

A GOTHIC-STYLE oak dining chair with unusual pillar-shaped legs. This chair-back has also been carved in window-like shapes.

43

board doors. A mirror beside the entrance door has the same form of arched top as the rest of the furniture, and this is also echoed in the shape of the room window and door. Daylight streams through the stained glass window, but working flambeaux and a floor candelabra illuminate the room when the sun has gone.

On the back wall, in true baronial style, are a moose's head, a bear's head, and a pair of crossed swords. Below the picture on the mantelpiece are a splendid bronze and two candlesticks representing intertwined tree branches. Before the fire stands an intriguing device for roasting meat, and on the floor is a tiger skin rug. The plush, red velvet bedspread and drapes behind the head of the bed offer the only strong splash of color in the room. At the foot of the bed stands an old trunk with a candlestick and Bible resting on its lid.

This is a scene set within a room box measuring 19 inches (47cm) wide by 12 inches (30cm) deep and 14 inches (35cm) high. A false wall with space cut out for a fireplace has been built 1½ inches (4cm) out from the left-hand wall to create the chimney. An angled section of plywood has been glued across the opposite back corner to make a wall for the headboard. Shapes traced from the back of the dresser – which was bought ready-made – were drawn on one side of the room for a window and on the other for the door and then cut out.

After the ceiling had been primed and painted, the walls were clad with stone-block design sheeting from Reuben Barrows. The floor, too,

ABOVE

This suit of armor is actually plastic, but has been carefully painted to represent metal.

RIGHT

The complete room. The use of light coming in through the stained glass window is effective in creating the right atmosphere.

was fitted with a different design of the same type of covering. Once this was done, stairs to the door were constructed with blocks of styrofoam which had been chipped and sanded to look old and worn. When stuck together, they were covered with a layer of plaster crack-filler and then painted with different tones of gray to represent stone.

For the door 1/16-inch (1.5mm) basswood was cut into strips and reassembled to make a sheet about 3 × 7 inches (7.5 × 17.5cm). This was stained black and fitted with appropriate knobs and then glued behind the door space. Similarly, a piece of plastic stained glass was adapted to fit behind the window opening. Next a fireplace was glued into position, and the electrical flambeaux and five-arm candelabra –

both by Memories in Miniature – were wired in.

For the furniture, an ideally styled matching set was found. For this room to work, the furniture needed to be the same style. These pieces were produced by the Bespaq Company and were comparatively inexpensive. The brass knobs, mirrors, and fabrics were removed; each piece was given a light sanding to remove the varnish and then repainted. Once this was done, the brass knobs were replaced, mirrors put back, and the bed covered.

Apart from adding accessories that emphasize or enhance the style, it is sometimes interesting to give a sign of activity that has taken place within a room. Here, among the swords and daggers, trophy heads and tiger skin, a spilled cup is left at the bottom of the stairs.

ABOVE
One of a pair of stuffed and mounted trophies in the room. This moose's head is made by the Lawbre Company.

A REAL MEDIEVAL Gothic bedroom from Penhow Castle in Wales. These were just the sort of interiors that the Victorians looked to for inspiration. Note the thick stone walls and heavy wooden bed. The atmosphere is gloomy and would have been lit only by natural light and candles. The pointed arch of the door and the heavy wooden furniture are significant elements, which the Victorians later adopted to be part of their style.

ABOVE
A beautiful miniature bronze moose sculpted by craftsman Daniel Kronberg.

Mackintosh Bedroom

In 1902 W. W. Blackie, a Scottish publisher, commissioned Charles Rennie Mackintosh to design a house which was to be built on an open hillside near Helensburgh in Scotland. This miniature bedroom has been based on a guest bedroom from that house.

This room is typical of the style, having walls and a ceiling of white and a fitted carpet of cream wool. Above the bed, the curved ceiling forms an intimate cave effect, and the curved window area, which would look out over Scottish hillsides, also reflects this form.

ABOVE

Throughout the bedroom, the paintwork is white. The shutters with spyholes – reminiscent of old castle embrasures – the baseboards, the shelf above the bed, the door, architrave, and fireplace surround all are finished in white. The furniture, too, is completely white.

RIGHT

The lamp on this washstand is perhaps a little out of place, but the decorative Tiffany-style glass reflects the form and colors of the side panels next to the bed and gives out a soft warm light that reflects the quality of a Mackintosh room.

COMPLETING MOST OF his important works between approximately 1893 and 1911, Charles Rennie Mackintosh worked as an architect at a time when mass manufacture was well established. Some craftsmen and designers were rebelling against this mass production in a movement which promoted individual arts and crafts. These artists, who formed the Arts and Crafts Movement, looked back to the Middle Ages as the true age of the craftsperson. They took their inspiration from that time, combining it with natural themes of animals and plants. While fundamentally in sympathy with these ideas, Mackintosh had a much broader outlook, colored by strong influences from his own Scottish background. He incorporated the Arts and Crafts ideals into his work, but used them in a way which has made them suitable for the practicality of the twentieth century.

Mackintosh was also an artist, and through his study of plants he produced stylized versions which appeared as watercolors and which are also recurring themes in his interior designs. Essentially an architect, he believed, however, that the interior of a building was as important in its overall design as the exterior. This is the premise from which his interior designs

stemmed. Mackintosh's work was unique and is now instantly recognizable and highly prized.

To recreate his style, look carefully at the pieces he made. He used high-backed chairs, cabinets with doors closed by organic-shaped fastenings, built-in closets, and cozy corner settles, often against plain white walls. For both walls and furnishings, surface decoration was minimal – usually in the form of a stylized plant stem or flower. These floral, growing forms were carved into tall, sinewy structures on both furniture and buildings. The colors most often used for this type of decoration were soft pink, gray, beige, and green. Flooring was plain and uncluttered.

All the furniture in this miniature room is made by Scottish miniature craftsman, Ian Holoran, and is a true representation of Mackintosh's work. The bed, covered with an off-white spread, is set in the alcove beneath the vaulted ceiling and on each side leaded, stained glass panels in stylized plant shapes rise

LEFT
The grate looks well-used in this splendid Mackintosh model made by top craftsman Peter Mattinson.

A MACKINTOSH FIREPLACE from the Hunterian Museum in Glasgow. The metal panel was originally part of a firescreen made in 1899 by Margaret MacDonald. You can see how accurately the miniature matches the original.

to reach the rail. In the foreground stands a splendid cheval mirror, painted white. This has small carved tulip heads at the top and a series of small glass insets. The high-backed chair in the window is instantly recognizable and epitomizes the Mackintosh style. This chair is more geometric than the other pieces in the room, having a less organic quality.

The washstand, too, is geometric, but incorporates the same organic shapes in its carved decoration as appear on both the bed and mirror. Mackintosh's design for the fireplace in this room is inspirational. The panel set above the fire would have been of metal and was probably

taken from an original by Margaret MacDonald, Mackintosh's wife.

From the main room, the door on the left offers a glimpse of a room or hallway beyond. In total contrast to the all-white bedroom, this area is dark. Beside an open cabinet, which incorporates flowing forms and stencil work, stand two high-backed chairs, perhaps the most easily-recognized of Mackintosh designs. These are perfect examples of geometric forms used together with organic carved decoration. There is also a large chair, originally a design for the Willow Tea Rooms in Glasgow, and an oval center table of hardwood. All these pieces have been designed and made by Mackintosh furniture specialists Felton Miniatures.

These two rooms could well be set within a dollhouse, perhaps on an upstairs floor. The room boxes were made of new plywood and, to achieve a good interior finish, the wood was first lightly sanded and then painted with a coat of primer. To make the arch above the bed, a thin piece of basswood was cut as a former and glued in place. This in turn had a piece of cardboard bent within it to form the curved surface which was glued to the side and back walls. When the primer was dry and all the cracks carefully filled in, the whole room was given two coats of flat white latex paint. For the door, a plain piece of wood was cut 2½ × 6½ inches (6 × 16cm), and a frame was made for it from miniature architraving. A hole was then cut in the wall for the door. When installed, the frame and architrave were given a coat of satin finish latex, and a purchased door handle was sprayed silver and glued in the appropriate place. A further hole was cut in the wall to accommodate the fireplace. The carpet is made from a piece of dressmaker's velvet, stretched smooth and thinly glued around the edges.

For baseboards, strips of wood were painted and stuck in afterward, as was the shelf below the arch above the bed. Below this, two stained glass side-screens from Becky Saxe-Falstein are set into position.

The ceiling light was crafted by Peter Mattinson. This type of light appears in the Willow Tea Rooms, Glasgow, and again is instantly recognizable as Mackintosh style. The wires from it and the lamp on the washstand

BELOW

The beautiful, white-painted, high-backed chair, together with the miniature cheval mirror, are both the work of Ian Holoran.

were pushed through tiny holes drilled in the ceiling and wall respectively and connected to a transformer behind.

The pieces of furniture commissioned from Ian Holoran were then placed in their correct locations. The bed was covered with a thick cotton spread. Although, not exactly faithful to the original, a lamp, pitcher, and bowl were found for the washstand and suitable pieces of china for the cabinet in the side room.

In the second room, scale wallpaper was used, pasted to the primed wood surface with ordinary wallpaper paste. From a scale parquet-block flooring sheet, an accurately measured piece the size of the floor was cut out and glued in.

LEFT
This dark, wooden, open cabinet in Mackintosh style is produced by Felton Miniatures.

LEFT
The dark inner room or hallway features pieces of furniture by Felton Miniatures.

ABOVE
Dark wooden table with a Mackintosh-inspired book made by Becky Saxe-Falstein.

New York Apartment

E clecticism is the choice and selection of things that please you, whatever their style or origin. A blend of modern and antique furniture can be skillfully put together to create an interesting and completely individual style for the 1990s. In this miniature setting, we imagine that a New York designer has cleverly mixed a variety of modern and antique objects and furniture to make an intriguing, contemporary living space.

Today, in so many ways, we draw on the past just as much as the Victorians did and want to combine the best of all styles. Nevertheless, many of us live in modest homes with limited living space available, so for us rooms must serve many purposes and furniture required for assorted needs must work well together. Contrasting styles of furniture, when considered carefully for color, finish, and form, can be placed side by side in a happy blend of favorite items.

An interior of the mid-1990s is one of easy comfort. We enjoy carpeted floors, central heating, large windows, and electric lighting. In either a new or old building, we live in a modern world. Being surrounded with items to suit our own personal taste, we create rooms as expressions of ourselves. Furniture can be modern, Art Deco or classical. Objects often reflect

To decorate the room, an overall color scheme was chosen, and the variety of tones within it was carefully followed. The floor is a warm, golden parquet and the wallpaper a yellowy cream. Paintwork and lampshades are pale cream to blend in.

The Art Deco sofa and round coffee table are made by French miniature artisan Laurence Disle after the French designer Emile Jacques Rhulmann. The sofa is beautifully upholstered in leather representing tiger skin, and the coffee table is of a rare wood with superb white bone detailing. Upon it stands warm-colored glassware by American artist Francis Whitmore in the style of Tiffany, while the small Art Deco bookends and figurines have been made by Englishman Neil Carter. On the right-hand wall stands an intricately carved table made of wood. This has been carefully

ABOVE

A beautiful Rhulmann-style, leather-covered sofa by French artist Laurence Disle.

personal interests – a piano for a musician, a desk for a writer, and so on. This thinking makes for eclectic rooms.

Our designer has considered his needs from his living space in downtown Manhattan and has created a room of great individuality and style scaled down to one inch to the foot (1:12 scale).

The spirit of the Art Deco period has been interpreted in an original and individual manner and has been set alongside Chippendale chairs and a rococo-style table. Use your imagination to picture the characters who might live in this stylish apartment.

gilded and its top, *faux* painted to resemble marble, displays silverware by silversmith Terence Stringer. Above this table, a cast metal mirror frame has also been carefully gilded.

Flanking the table are two gilt Chippendale chairs, made from kits, which have been up-holstered with 1920s ribbon. The screen is also a kit and is faced with a *trompe l'oeil* painting from American-based artist Natasha.

In total contrast, toward the center of the room stands a mass-produced clavichord and matching stool which have been spray-painted in gloss black; these are set off by a group of poppies placed in a pot.

Picture frames match the wood of the sofa and table, and bronzes are used as ornaments on both sides of the room. A plant stands beside the open fire, and more silver is placed on the desk. The warm tones of the wood blend happily

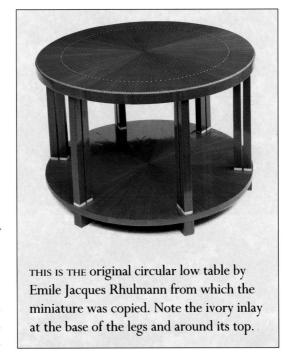

THIS IS THE original circular low table by Emile Jacques Rhulmann from which the miniature was copied. Note the ivory inlay at the base of the legs and around its top.

LEFT
The complete New York apartment living room.

55

with the colder glint and shine of metal, and the furniture provides a whole range of color combinations. This is a room for a variety of uses and houses a collection of objects that work in total harmony with each other.

The setting for an eclectic style is almost immaterial and is certainly not confined to that of a living room. However, the building that one might suppose houses this apartment would probably be from the 1930s. The shape and size of the room have been based on this assumption and therefore reflects room proportions of that era.

As before, within the space, false walls have been cut for the back, chimney breast, and the wall that contains the entrance door. Before fitting them in, apertures were made to hold two French windows in the back, the single door, and the fireplace. A black-painted liner was constructed for the fire interior and its floor set with a sliver of marble.

Once this was done, the ceiling was painted off-white, and when this dried, the walls were papered. With the pre-painted door frames in position, a sheet of Reuben Barrows parquet flooring was measured and laid in place. The baseboard was painted in advance and then mitered to fit all around the room. For lighting, a fluorescent tube was mounted on the wall at the back of the space behind the French windows. By turning it on or off, the effects of day or night respectively can be achieved. Inside the room, shaded wall lights were wired through holes in the wall and connected to a transformer.

The cord to the table lamp runs underneath the floor to connect with the rest of the lamps.

Such a project provides a great opportunity to experiment with all kinds of new techniques. In the early stages, an object or piece of furniture that does not reach your expectation can easily be rejected in favor of another. The flexibility of the style means that no single piece of furniture is essential to the whole. For example, the original idea for this miniature included a console table which was to stand between the French windows. It was to be of cardboard, subsequently sandpapered and *faux* painted to look like colored, grained wood. The result was a great disappointment, having been rather badly executed, and the piece looked too stark against the wall. The final cabinet used here was much easier to construct. It was made of wood, and experiments with paint stippled on with a sponge worked well. A small sheet of brass mesh with fabric behind it completed a much more interesting piece.

Gilding is a technique that gives a satisfying result. On the chairs, pictures, and mirror frames and on the ornate side table, this process was used. Although it is possible to use gold paint, the staged gilding method used here provided a much more pleasing finish.

Once the gilding on the side table base was dry, a three-part marbling kit was tested on its top. This, too, worked well. The chairs are English-made kits available from *International Dolls' House News*; their backs and legs were gilded, then the seats were upholstered before assembly. The screen was made from a kit by D. Anne Ruff. The directions were followed closely until the paint stage. After that, a sheet of miniature *trompe l'oeil* was cut and mounted onto the screen, and small metal buttons were then glued at its top.

As a rule, gloss paint is too unreal for a miniature, but to spray the clavichord and stool in gloss black seemed like a challenge, and this time it worked.

Finally, prints were chosen for the frames, and the velvet was carefully cut for the carpet. Then the whole set could be put together – purchased furniture alongside saved treasures – much in the way you would arrange furniture in your own home.

BELOW
A gilded Chippendale chair made from a kit with a desk made by Denis Jenvey.

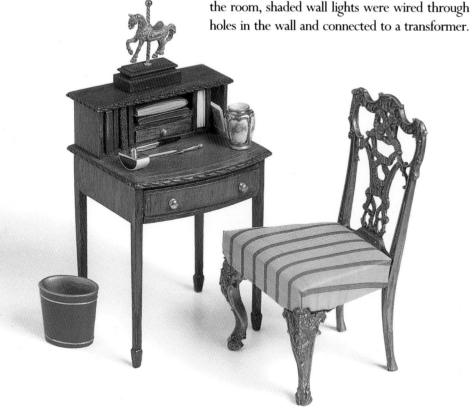

RIGHT

An ornate, carved side table that has been gilded and faux marbled, displaying beautiful silverware by Terence Stringer.

BELOW

The right-hand corner of the room showing the clavichord, trompe l'oeil screen, and gilded chairs and side table.

Monet's Dining Room

C laude Monet was born in Paris in 1840. He spent his young life in Le Havre, and it was here he discovered the joys of painting directly from nature. In Paris he met Renoir, Sisley, and Bazille and in London in 1871 discovered Turner. It was at this time that his interest in and collection of Japanese engravings began. This unique interior features many such engravings and is a reflection of Monet's general taste. The miniature represents the general atmosphere as well as individual features from this lovely room.

N 1883, CLAUDE MONET settled in the small village of Giverny. In a house set beside the road and looking out onto a large orchard, he turned the single-story barn into his drawing room and studio. As time went by, he altered the garden, had flowers planted, and built three greenhouses. In 1895 he created the pools, water garden, and a Japanese bridge inspired by an engraving, and by 1900 he had completed a garage, a darkroom for photography, two further bedrooms, and a second gallery where he worked on the series of waterlily paintings which made him famous throughout the world.

For this miniature, inspiration has been taken from this beautiful home, specifically from one particular room: Monet's dining room. This is a room of unique individuality which still remains intact today. Painted in two shades of yellow, it displays the remaining pieces from Monet's Limoges dinner service, and other blue china fills large, glass-doored sideboards. The collection of engravings, started by Monet in 1871, by Japanese artists Utamaro, Hiroshige, Hoikusai, Sharaku, Kioyonaga, Shunsho, and Toyokuni are hung here, too, restored and re-framed as part of the restoration of the room that took place in 1966.

For the miniature, a double room box was used. Glorious sunshine yellows are the background that shows off the collection of blue and white china. Taking its directive from the house in Giverny, all of the furniture in this miniature version has been customized to re-create the theme. The floor is in two tones (brown and cream) and is made of real ceramic tiles, each of which had to be laid separately. The walls and ceiling have been painted pale flat yellow and the baseboards, paneling, chair

THE YELLOW DINING ROOM from Monet's home in Giverny where he lived from 1883 on. Note the decorative blue and white china and the original engravings on the wall.

rail, architrave, and cornice have been picked out in a deeper yellow gloss. The fireplace has been treated the same way.

On the back wall, mounted in black gloss frames, are miniature examples of the Japanese engravings that Monet collected. The plates on the walls are by expert miniature makers Terry Curran and Muriel Hopwood. Further examples of Muriel Hopwood's fine ceramic pieces are the lidded jars and plates on the sideboard and the plates and dishes in the glazed cabinet.

Through the open door of the main room, there is a view of the blue kitchen. This room is also based on one at Giverny. Here the walls are of assorted blue and white tiles, the curtains are of blue and white fabric, and the shelves and paintwork are also blue and white. The old stone sink and floor quarry tiles are lovely features, again all copied from the original kitchen.

Both the dining room and side kitchen of Monet's Giverny home have been recreated side by side in a large room box that now has a glass front within a frame to keep it protected from dust.

An interior wall with an internal door was fitted first, and then the whole interior received a coat of primer. This done, the walls and ceiling of the dining room were given two coats of pale yellow latex paint. At the same time, wood for the cornice, the door in its frame and the ready-made wainscoting and chair rail were sprayed with yellow gloss. After they were dry, the cornices and door assembly were glued into place, and the flat section of the wainscoting and chair rail were painted with the pale yellow latex, leaving the moldings in gloss.

These panels were then carefully mitered and positioned on the lower walls of the room. For the floor, two colors of 1-inch (2cm) square floor tiles by Terry Curran were glued down to form the required design. It was necessary to trim some of these to fit around the edges.

Meanwhile, in the blue kitchen, the ceiling was painted white, the floor was covered with Reuben Barrows's quarry-tile sheeting, and the walls were papered with a blue tile-patterned paper. After this, pre-painted baseboard and a false door were glued in.

ABOVE
The china cabinet, with its doors open to show the fine miniature porcelain work of artist Muriel Hopwood.

61

LEFT
The corner of the miniature room features the glazed china cabinet which has its doors closed.

ABOVE
The complete miniature dining room.

OPPOSITE
The blue and white kitchen showing the flat stone sink.

BELOW
Yellow-painted furniture with porcelain lidded jars by Muriel Hopwood.

Next came the furniture. As the furniture used in the real house in Giverny had been painted one color, obviously the same approach was used in the miniature. Relatively inexpensive pieces were chosen, matching as closely as possible the style of the real furniture. From these, the knobs and glazing were removed, and they were all given a thorough sanding. In the case of the side table and glazed cabinet, some of the carving was reshaped to match the original more accurately. This done, the table and chairs, cabinet, sideboard, wall mirror, and fireplace were all sprayed with yellow gloss paint and then touched up using pale yellow latex. The fireplace received a trim of Terry Curran's edge-tiles, and the table and chairs were upholstered with small-scale gingham fabric. Curtains of a similar fabric were also made for the kitchen.

As with the lighting in the other miniature rooms, wires were run to central points on the ceilings of the dining room and kitchen and one was run through the back wall for a table lamp shaped in traditional oil-lamp style. While all manner of 12-volt miniature light fittings can be bought, one suitable for the interpretation of Giverny failed to turn up. Eventually one was made from a section of a plastic sphere with miniature castings glued on as decoration.

Reduced color photocopies were taken from a catalog of Japanese engravings and were framed with black-painted moldings. They were then hung on the wall.

Finally, the room was furnished with the freshly painted pieces and a vase of flowers set on the table. Some wonderful greenish ceramic ware was found to match that on the fireplace, and Muriel Hopwood's fine blue and white porcelain was spread through the rest of the room.

Bauhaus Room

The Bauhaus movement produced furniture designed for minimalistic living and included angular shapes and primary colors. Walls were plain and built-in furniture was geometric. New, light materials like chrome and stainless steel were used. In this miniature, you can recognize the origins of the style in the tubular chrome chairs and glass-topped table, the leather-upholstered seating, and cube-formed storage units. Taking as its basis furniture conforming to the Bauhaus ideals and grouping them with various Art Deco pieces, this is an interior that could well have existed in the 1920s.

RIGHT

The complete interior. The large display storage unit against the back wall houses a number of pieces from the Art Deco period. There are small figurines influenced by the Ballet Russe and a cocktail shaker by silversmith Terence Stringer.

ABOVE

This glass-topped table displays a silver Art Deco candle holder and a fruit bowl by Jeff Wise, and miniature flatware pieces by Ken Palmer.

I N 1919 IN Weimar in Germany, the Bauhaus was founded by architect Walter Gropius for the teaching of art, design, and architecture to produce complete living works of art. As with the Arts and Crafts Movement, mechanization and mass production were blamed for the removal of the craft element from design. The aim of the school was to harmonize craft roots with the manufacturing process. Many artists and designers were attracted to the school, and workshops designed and experimented with both old and new materials. This was the opportunity to throw away old ideals and unnecessary ornamentation in design and produce design dictated by function.

Having stripped away superficial decoration and redundant, irrelevant shapes in design, linear geometric forms emerged. The style we now know as Bauhaus emerged from this. Buildings were clean and rectilinear; furniture was functionally basic; tools and equipment geometric and usable.

Curiously, while the Bauhaus taught its ideals of truth from 1920–33, in almost direct opposition, in 1925 an array of extravagantly decorated arts was shown in an Exhibition des Arts Decoratifs in Paris, France. Inspired by these, artists and designers across the globe exploded in a glorious celebration of experimentation in new materials and mass production. Ironically, among the wealth of influences, the Bauhaus featured strongly.

In this miniature room, walls and carpet are mainly in two shades of pink, and the dining area is set on a raised platform of light stripwood flooring. This is surrounded by wallpaper of an

A MODERN INTERIOR with tubular chrome chairs and a glass-topped table. Although this is from the 1990s, its roots in the ideas that emerged from the Bauhaus can easily be seen.

67

ABOVE

Famous for her work in Art Deco style was the pottery designer Clarice Cliff. Within a glazed section of the cabinet are miniature representations of her work by both Muriel Hopwood and Patricia Venning.

BELOW

Degas girl dancer by miniature sculptor Neil Carter.

Art Deco geometric design. French maker Pierre Mourey constructed the dining table and chairs from aluminum tubing and stainless steel wire, very much in the Bauhaus style.

The silver ice bucket in true Art Deco style rests on a base symbolizing a cascading waterfall design. The torchère, too, is typical Art Deco. Both these pieces are produced by craftsman Jeff Wise. Standing on a plinth is a beautiful model of a Degas girl dancer. This together with figurines on the shelf are the work of miniature sculptor Neil Carter. On the left-hand wall, a soft black sofa of real leather is framed by two halogen uplighters, all by Pierre Mourey.

The very nature of a Bauhaus theme is that it should be rectilinear. It is very fitting then that this room has been set in a simple plywood box! It was primed and painted pale pink, and then the Art Deco-style foil paper was pasted into place. To form the raised platform, a

¾-inch (18mm) thick piece of plywood was cut into a triangle with one side curved and the two straight, to fit into the room corner. The outer edge of this was painted to match the walls and the top surface covered with a sheet of miniature wood planking. This was sanded, stained, and varnished to achieve the right effect, and the platform was glued in position. A piece of velvet carpeting from Pitty Pat Designs was then cut and fitted to the rest of the floor.

Once the basics of construction were complete, the one-piece storage unit by Pierre Mourey of Le Bouffon du Roy was sited on the raised section behind the dining table and chairs.

Selected items were grouped together and displayed on the shelves and dining table, and a special plinth of plastic stippled with gray and pink paint was made to display Neil Carter's model of the Degas girl dancer. To complete the scene, a simple poster picture by Kandinsky was cut out of a catalog and attached to the wall.

Santa Fe Store

From the Southwest of America, descriptions such as Spanish, Navajo, California, or simply Southwestern no longer quite capture the spirit of the style that is now known as Santa Fe. The town of Santa Fe is, of course, in New Mexico, and the rich colors and the soft tones and textures of the desert have influenced this style.

The original inhabitants of the region, the southwestern Native Americans, have a unique and colorful culture. The designs of this culture are a living part of the arts and crafts of the American Indian today. They have played a major part in influencing the development of Santa Fe style.

Over the years Native Americans, while preserving their own cultural traditions in their work, have also utilized new influences and materials. Today their designs are well recognized for the use of traditional art forms in the making of silver items decorated with turquoise, beautiful bead work, small carvings, wood carvings, pottery, basketweaving, cloth and rug weaving, and paintings.

Now all these influences have played a large part in forming a new interior design style adapted for modern-day living – Sante Fe style. Against backgrounds of vibrant turquoise, brilliant terracotta, the colors of the desert sands and sun-bleached wood, stand modern furniture pieces in harmony with traditional Southwestern arts and crafts. A feeling of the sun and desert is all-important here. Rooms in this style should be light, bright, and warm. White is usually used for walls and floors, with shades of terracotta, turquoise, and sandy yellow to set the scene. Furniture takes on the light tones of driftwood, while pots, lamps, and ornaments reflect the influence of Native American arts and crafts.

BELOW
A display unit of hardwood and glass showing Kachina dolls by Little White Dove and pots and drums by Rainbow Hand.

LEFT

The complete store full of
furniture, lamps, rugs,
and pottery. The cash
desk is under the stairs.

ABOVE

A separate armchair by
Taos Sun Miniatures.

Set in a new shopping plaza somewhere in southern California, this furniture store in miniature displays the very essence of the style. Outside, the open courtyard would be alive with busy shoppers as locals and tourists alike enjoy the ambience of the attractive Spanish-influenced architecture.

Inside the store, the walls are roughly textured and painted in shades of white, terracotta, and sand. Floors are bare-boarded and terracotta-tiled. These tiles match those of the courtyard and sidewalks outside.

Around the store furniture, lighting, dishes, and baskets are all worked in Santa Fe style. On a display shelf unit of hardwood and glass, the fine crafts of miniature makers Little White Dove and Rainbow Hand can be seen. Tradi-

MODERN ITEMS IN the Santa Fe style including a small Navajo rug, a rattle of wood and feathers, and an earthenware candle holder.

RIGHT
The stairs leading to the upper-floor balcony of the store.

tional crafts are displayed in the form of drums, a violin, an array of Kachina dolls, pottery, rattles, and a pair of moccasins.

In the center of the room, furniture is grouped in a homey setting – as is often the case in furniture stores. The sofa and chair have Navajo-patterned cushions and, in the same sun-bleached gray wood, there is a coffee table to match. The cabinet with open doors in the corner matches this set as well and displays more American Indian artifact pieces. Further small tables are also to be found.

Built of plywood, this furniture store is in fact part of a complete miniature scene. With all components assembled, it measures a generous 7 feet 2 inches (2.2m) long by 19 inches (47.5cm) deep and 21 inches (52.5cm) high. However, the store is half of a section that also contains the courtyard.

The exterior was finished by stippling on latex paint mixed with a small amount of plaster filler. The roof tiles were cut from a finished sheet made by Reuben Barrows and stuck to the outside surface with white glue. Inside, after priming, white latex was painted on the ceiling. For the walls, latex in terracotta, white, and sand colors was applied.

Having fitted in a wooden gallery and some assembled railings, a ready-made staircase was put in position and painted. Next came the floors. For the front section, terracotta stone tiles which matched those already used in the courtyard were chosen. These are made by Houseworks and come in sheets on net backing which means they can be cut and trimmed to shape. After gluing them in place, the cracks must be grouted.

At the back of the store and up on the balconies, further sheeting by Reuben Barrows was cut to shape and glued down. This time the design chosen was a light wood plank boarding.

Next came the wiring. Wires from the table lamps – which were made by Dragonfly – and the wall cabinet were all run through to the back of the box and linked to those that run from the ceiling light. These in turn were connected to the transformer.

Once the construction work was complete, it then remained to arrange the furniture and the assembled accessories. With a project such

as this, where lots of different items are required, it is best, if possible, to start making the collection well in advance. Often it can be a collection of objects of the same type that sparks off the idea for a scheme in the first place.

In this case, most of the pieces were bought in the style required in advance of the making of the miniature in Santa Fe style. However, extra plain wood shelving (and the odd accessory) was brought into service and painted in appropriate colors.

When a number of intricate pieces are involved in a display of this nature, it is usually advisable to place larger pieces of furniture at the back of the room and then work forward with smaller items at the front, setting out the accessories as you go. This is a general guide that applies to all miniatures.

ABOVE

The courtyard outside the miniature store. In the center is an ornamental fountain, and a flower stand enlivens the white wall. Here pedestrians stroll or rest in the shade of the palm trees overhead.

73

BELOW

A miniature Santa Fe-style coffee table.

Biedermeier Study

Taste in interior decoration never has stood still. Life continually moves forward, and social changes bring about different desires, needs, and tastes. In England at the beginning of the nineteenth century, life became less formal. Rooms were smaller, and furniture was grouped more intimately. Neoclassiscism was in vogue, introducing shapes and forms from ancient Egypt, Rome, and Greece. These influences can be seen clearly in the furniture and ornaments that are part of the Biedermeier style which developed in the early 1800s.

RIGHT
Biedermeier-style china cabinet containing a bowl by Ron Benson, a silver urn sold by Peter Aquisto, and a repainted antique jasper pot.

I N FRANCE, NAPOLEON'S military campaigns in Egypt heralded a new French style. France was the center of Napoleon's expanding empire at the start of the nineteenth century and here, together with the growth of classicism, imperial motifs became a part of the style of the time.

After the defeat of Napoleon in 1815, there was a great reaction in Europe against the pretentious grandeur of the Napoleonic empire. Although the Austrians and Germans were also using classical motifs, their versions of the style were much less flamboyant than those displayed in France. Their emphasis was on solidity, comfort, and function. The term Biedermeier was given to the style later on, after it had become well-established, and originated from a fictional character "Paper Biedermeier" who epitomized middle-class bourgeois ideals.

The more functional Germanic interpretation of the style employed light woods like maple, birch, and cherry. Ornamentation was kept to a minimum and room settings were kept simple, low-level, and stylish. Floors were often bare wood – parquet or just plain boards – and curtains and upholstery a simple white.

To make a miniature room, thought must be given to what the important aspects are that will best interpret the style. In this room several pieces of furniture are grouped together. A round table with chairs is set before a sofa in the center of the room. To the right, a chair is placed before a functional desk. China cabinets

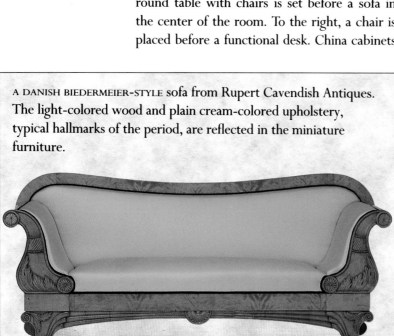

A DANISH BIEDERMEIER-STYLE sofa from Rupert Cavendish Antiques. The light-colored wood and plain cream-colored upholstery, typical hallmarks of the period, are reflected in the miniature furniture.

and bookcases for storage and display were popular, all in light woods and using curved forms, and these too are represented here in the miniature. Pictures are hung fairly low and in small groupings. Above all, it is the contrast of the light wood with black detail that immediately denotes the Biedermeier style.

Made entirely from miniature kits in the Biedermeier style, each piece of furniture used here has been stained and varnished for an authentic look. In the fashion of the time, the table is placed in front of the sofa, and other chairs are set around it. On the left is a tall glazed cabinet with ebony side pillars. This, too, is highly typical of the style, and it displays a china bowl by craftsman Ron Benson and a splendid silver piece from Peter Aquisto. On the right is a most elaborate writing desk, again typical of the Biedermeier style. This has drawers at the bottom and at the top, and there are ten small drawers behind the desk flap, which opens down to reveal them. Standing on top of this piece is one of five busts which are dotted around the room and flanking it are two urns, again made by Ron Benson.

In front of the well-dressed window is a delicate window seat with ebony inlay. Beside this stands a tall bookcase which again has ebony columns. Across the room a semicircular wall table can be seen with a mirror above it. This, too, has the ubiquitous turned ebony pillars.

In keeping with true Biedermeier style, the floor is made of parquet blocks with a small rose-patterned rug upon it. Pictures are grouped together, and their frames are light elm wood, ebony or gilt. All are hung fairly low on the wall. Wallpapers are striped and blend well with the wood. The upholstery is cream and so are the curtains, which are edged with gold braid and tassels.

LEFT
The complete Biedermeier gentleman's study with its selection of items, all made from miniature kits.

77

*The Biedermeier bookcase
full of books with pages
that turn, a speciality of
Carol Wenk Miniatures.*

A REAL BIEDERMEIER interior styled by
Rupert Cavendish Antiques. It includes a
German secretaire, a birchwood sofa, an
armchair, and a stool, all of which were
made between 1820 and 1830.

To complete the room, there is a cornice
around the ceiling with a matched wood baseboard and picture rail. Through the curtain to
the left can be seen a small rest area, furnished
with a sleigh bed, a bedside cabinet, and a chest
of drawers.

This miniature room was part of a central
floor in a modern dollhouse. To accommodate
it, an interior wall was removed and a wider
doorway cut into the remaining one. The side
window was also enlarged to justify the use of
a more dramatic window dressing.

In order to avoid electrical installation which
would disturb the rooms above and below, it
was a simple task to run the wires from table
lamps through small holes drilled in the back
wall. Remember it is always more effective to
mount light fixtures toward the back of a room
where natural light from the outside does not
reach.

After the cornice was mitered and attached
to the ceiling, two coats of latex paint were

ABOVE

*An elegant side table on
which sit two china urns
and a bronze bust.*

applied to the ceiling, cornice, and about 2 inches (5cm) down the wall. The remainder of the wall was then papered, and a pre-stained and varnished baseboard and picture rail were mitered and glued into place.

For the floor, a parquet design was chosen from Reuben Barrows' selection of sheeting and was trimmed and fitted into position.

After the designer had researched the correct styling for this room, curtains were commissioned from Lyntel to fit the window and also for the archway through to the rest area.

All the furniture was made from Mini Mundus kits, which produces a series in this style. Always follow kit instructions closely and remember that careful sandpapering is most important both for construction and final finish. These kits can be stained any color, but in this case cherry was chosen. The upright columns and decoration on the chair backs were painted flat black and then varnished. Choosing fabrics for upholstery can be tricky. Natural fibers work best, and those that are not too bulky are ideal for working in a small scale.

To match the curtains, the sofa, dining chairs, and window seat were covered in white silk, and the sofa bolsters were given small brass lion heads as a finishing touch. Once the furniture was assembled, accessories were chosen: busts, books, urns, and pictures all seemed appropriate for this study. Again, prints or photographs in keeping with the theme were cut out and mounted in ready-made frames. They were stuck to the wall using sticky mounting tack that allows adjustments to be made without harming the walls. This material is available through miniature specialist stores.

Finally, a printed rug was centered on the floor and the furniture and *objects d'art* positioned, producing an accurate total look.

ABOVE

A single Biedermeier-style chair made from a Mini Mundus kit.

79

LEFT

The right-hand side of the miniature shows the elegance of the white curtains, which were specially commissioned for the interior.

Miniatures Specialists

USA

Aquisto Silver
8901 O Suna Road NE
Albuquerque, NM 87111

Ron Benson
P.O. Box 5231
Richmond, VA 23220

J. Getzan
1935 S. Plus Grove Road
#350
Palatine, IL 60067

Lawbre Company
888 Tower Road
Mundelein, IL 60060

Little White Dove
7556 Union N.E.
Albuquerque, NM 87109

Natasha
106 Pinehurst Avenue
#A–42
New York, NY 10033

The Oldhams
5962 Sierra Drive
Redding, CA 96003

Rainbow Hand
Mini Moons Ago
4420A Catlin Circle
Carpinteria, CA 93013

D. Anne Ruff
1100 Vagabond Lane
Plymouth, MN 55447

Sir Thomas Thumb
1398 Oregon Road
Leola, PA 17540

Taos Sun
P.O. Box 2907
Taos, NM 87571

**Carol Wenk
Miniatures**
P.O. Box 770554
Lakewood, OH 44107

Francis Whittemore
480 Wade Avenue
Lansdale, PA 19446

UK

R. V. Barrows
30 Wolsey Gardens
Hainault
Essex
IG6 2SN

Blackwells
733 London Road
Westcliff-on-Sea
Essex
SS0 9ST

Busy Fingers
12 Samaritan Close
Benbush
Crawley
West Sussex
RH11 6BW

Neil Carter
55 Knox Road
Wellingborough
Northamptonshire
NN8 1JA

Felton Miniatures
Field Cottage
Elsthorpe Road
Stainfield
Lincolnshire
PE10 0RS

Ian Holoran
31 Turleum Road
Crieff
Perthshire
PH7 3QF

Muriel Hopwood
41 Eastbourne Avenue
Hodge Hill
Birmingham
B34 6AR

**Charlotte Hunt
Miniatures**
31 Westover Road
London
SW18 2RE

**International Dolls'
House News**
P.O. Box 154
Cobham
Surrey
KT11 2YE

The Lincolns
12 Studley Road
Harrogate
North Yorkshire
HG1 5JU

Lyntel
141 Watling Street
Park Street
St. Albans
Hertfordshire
AL2 2NN

Peter Mattinson
100 Stockton Lane
York
Yorkshire
YO3 0BU

**Memories in
Miniature**
Biddisham Lane
Biddisham
Somerset
BS26 2RG

Ken Palmer
The Courtyard
Pipe Grange Farm
Lichfield Road
Pipe Hill
Lichfield
Staffordshire
WS13 8JP

Becky Saxe-Falstein
37 The Copse
Fareham
Hampshire
PO15 6EG

Simply Shaker
86 Oaklands Avenue
Watford
Hertfordshire
WD1 4LW

Stokesay Ware
37 Sandbrook Road
Stoke Newington
London
N16 0SH

Terence Stringer
Spindles
Lexham Road
Litcham
Norfolk
PE32 2QQ

Sussex Crafts
Hassocks House
Comptons Browcane
Horsham
West Sussex
RH13 6BX

Pat Venning
Pineways
Faircross Avenue
Weymouth
Dorset
DT4 0DD

FRANCE

Laurence Disle
20 bis, rue Jacoucet
92210 Saint-Cloud

P. Mourey
33 avenue de Saint Cloud
78000 Versailles

The following makes of
miniatures are not
available directly from
the suppliers, but can be
found in specialist
outlets:

Bespaq Corporation

**Dragonfly
   International**

House Works

**D. P. Kronburg
   Miniature Statuary**

Mini Mundus

**Northeastern Scale
   Models Inc.**

Pitty Pat Designs

J. Wise